Simple. Clean. No Distractions

April

Monday
27

Tuesday
28

Wednesday
29

Thursday
30

Friday
1

Saturday
2

Sunday
3

May

Monday
4

Tuesday
5

Wednesday
6

Thursday
7

Friday
8

Saturday
9

Sunday
10

May

Monday
11

Tuesday
12

Wednesday
13

Thursday
14

Friday
15

Saturday
16

Sunday
17

May

Monday

18

Tuesday

19

Wednesday

20

Thursday

21

Friday

22

Saturday

23

Sunday

24

May

Monday
25

Tuesday
26

Wednesday
27

Thursday
28

Friday
29

Saturday
30

Sunday
31

June

Monday
1

Tuesday
2

Wednesday
3

Thursday
4

Friday
5

Saturday
6

Sunday
7

Month

Monday
8

Tuesday
9

Wednesday
10

Thursday
11

Friday
12

Saturday
13

Sunday
14

June

Monday
15

Tuesday
16

Wednesday
17

Thursday
18

Friday
19

Saturday	**Sunday**
20	21

June

Monday
22

Tuesday
23

Wednesday
24

Thursday
25

Friday
26

Saturday
27

Sunday
28

June

Monday
29

Tuesday
30

Wednesday
1

Thursday
2

Friday
3

Saturday
4

Sunday
5

July

Monday
6

Tuesday
7

Wednesday
8

Thursday
9

Friday
10

Saturday
11

Sunday
12

July

Monday
13

Tuesday
14

Wednesday
15

Thursday
16

Friday
17

Saturday
18

Sunday
19

July

Monday
20

Tuesday
21

Wednesday
22

Thursday
23

Friday
24

Saturday
25

Sunday
26

July

Monday
27

Tuesday
28

Wednesday
29

Thursday
30

Friday
31

Saturday
1

Sunday
2

August

Monday
3

Tuesday
4

Wednesday
5

Thursday
6

Friday
7

Saturday
8

Sunday
9

August

Monday

10

Tuesday

11

Wednesday

12

Thursday

13

Friday

14

Saturday	**Sunday**
15	16

August

Monday
17

Tuesday
18

Wednesday
19

Thursday
20

Friday
21

Saturday
22

Sunday
23

August

Monday
24

Tuesday
25

Wednesday
26

Thursday
27

Friday
28

Saturday
29

Sunday
30

August

Monday
31

Tuesday
1

Wednesday
2

Thursday
3

Friday
4

Saturday
5

Sunday
6

September

Monday
7

Tuesday
8

Wednesday
9

Thursday
10

Friday
11

Saturday
12

Sunday
13

September

Monday
14

Tuesday
15

Wednesday
16

Thursday
17

Friday
18

Saturday
19

Sunday
20

September

Monday
21

Tuesday
22

Wednesday
23

Thursday
24

Friday
25

Saturday
26

Sunday
27

September

Monday
28

Tuesday
29

Wednesday
30

Thursday
1

Friday
2

Saturday
3

Sunday
4

October

Monday
5

Tuesday
6

Wednesday
7

Thursday
8

Friday
9

Saturday
10

Sunday
11

October

Monday
12

Tuesday
13

Wednesday
14

Thursday
15

Friday
16

Saturday
17

Sunday
18

October

Monday
19

Tuesday
20

Wednesday
21

Thursday
22

Friday
23

Saturday
24

Sunday
25

October

Monday
26

Tuesday
27

Wednesday
28

Thursday
29

Friday
30

Saturday
31

Sunday
1

November

Monday
2

Tuesday
3

Wednesday
4

Thursday
5

Friday
6

Saturday
7

Sunday
8

November

Monday
9

Tuesday
10

Wednesday
11

Thursday
12

Friday
13

Saturday
14

Sunday
15

November

Monday
16

Tuesday
17

Wednesday
18

Thursday
19

Friday
20

Saturday
21

Sunday
22

November

Monday
23

Tuesday
24

Wednesday
25

Thursday
26

Friday
27

Saturday	**Sunday**
28	29

November

Monday
30

Tuesday
1

Wednesday
2

Thursday
3

Friday
4

Saturday
5

Sunday
6

December

Monday
7

Tuesday
8

Wednesday
9

Thursday
10

Friday
11

Saturday
12

Sunday
13

December

Monday
14

Tuesday
15

Wednesday
16

Thursday
17

Friday
18

Saturday
19

Sunday
20

December

Monday
21

Tuesday
22

Wednesday
23

Thursday
24

Friday
25

Saturday
26

Sunday
27

December

Monday
28

Tuesday
29

Wednesday
30

Thursday
31

Friday
1

Saturday
2

Sunday
3